T0390059

SilverTip

Physical Fitness

by Ashley Kuehl

Consultant: Caitlin Krieck, Social Studies Teacher and
Instructional Coach, The Lab School of Washington

BEARPORT
PUBLISHING

Minneapolis, Minnesota

Credits

Cover and title page, © Gorodenkoff/Adobe Stock; 3, © irin-k/Shutterstock; 5, © Lopolo/Shutterstock; 7, © 2xSamara.com/Shutterstock; 9, © SEBASTIAN KAULITZKI/SCIENCE PHOTO LIBRARY/Getty Images; 11, © MDV Edwards/Shutterstock; 13, © Marcos Elihu Castillo Ramirez/iStock; 15, © Jose Ignacio Martin Del Barco/iStock; 17, © fizkes/Shutterstock; 19, © Ground Picture/Shutterstock; 21, © Drazen Zigic/Shutterstock; 23, © AYO Production/Shutterstock; 25, © MENG KONGSAK/Shutterstock; 27, © ti-ja/iStock.

Bearport Publishing Company Product Development Team

Publisher: Jen Jenson; Director of Product Development: Spencer Brinker; Editorial Director: Allison Juda; Editor: Cole Nelson; Editor: Tiana Tran; Production Editor: Naomi Reich; Art Director: Kim Jones; Designer: Kayla Eggert; Designer: Steve Scheluchin; Production Specialist: Owen Hamlin

Statement on Usage of Generative Artificial Intelligence

Bearport Publishing remains committed to publishing high-quality nonfiction books. Therefore, we restrict the use of generative AI to ensure accuracy of all text and visual components pertaining to a book's subject. See BearportPublishing.com for details.

Library of Congress Cataloging-in-Publication Data

Names: Kuehl, Ashley, 1977– author.
Title: Physical fitness / by Ashley Kuehl.
Description: Silvertip books. | Minneapolis, Minnesota : Bearport Publishing Company, [2026] | Series: Health: need to know | Includes bibliographical references and index.
Identifiers: LCCN 2025001588 (print) | LCCN 2025001589 (ebook) | ISBN 9798895770757 (library binding) | ISBN 9798895775226 (paperback) | ISBN 9798895771921 (ebook)
Subjects: LCSH: Physical fitness–Juvenile literature. | Exercise–Juvenile literature.
Classification: LCC GV481 .K786 2026 (print) | LCC GV481 (ebook) | DDC 613.7/1–dc23/eng/20250210
LC record available at https://lccn.loc.gov/2025001588
LC ebook record available at https://lccn.loc.gov/2025001589

For more information, write to Bearport Publishing, 3500 American Blvd W, Suite 150, Bloomington, MN 55431.

Contents

Move a Little Faster

Exercise affects your whole body. During a jog, you feel your leg muscles working hard. Your breathing speeds up. So does your heartbeat. Your body gets warm, and you start to sweat. Exercise improves the body's physical fitness.

You can exercise in many ways. Playing team sports is a fun way to move. Carrying groceries and walking around the block are exercise, too.

Tip-Top Shape

Physical fitness is the ability of the body to do the everyday things it needs. People who are physically fit have plenty of energy. They can do their schoolwork and chores. They also have the energy for sports or other hobbies.

A physically fit person is less likely to get sick. They do not feel tired during the day. They also often have lower **stress** levels.

Bigger, Stronger, Faster

Physical fitness has three parts. The first part is strength. Strong muscles can easily move the body. Bones need strength, too. They support the body.

Exercise helps build strength in muscles and bones. Muscles get bigger when you exercise. Exercise also makes bones **denser**.

Muscles have to break down to build up. With hard exercise, muscles tear. Soon, they rebuild. This makes muscles bigger and stronger than before.

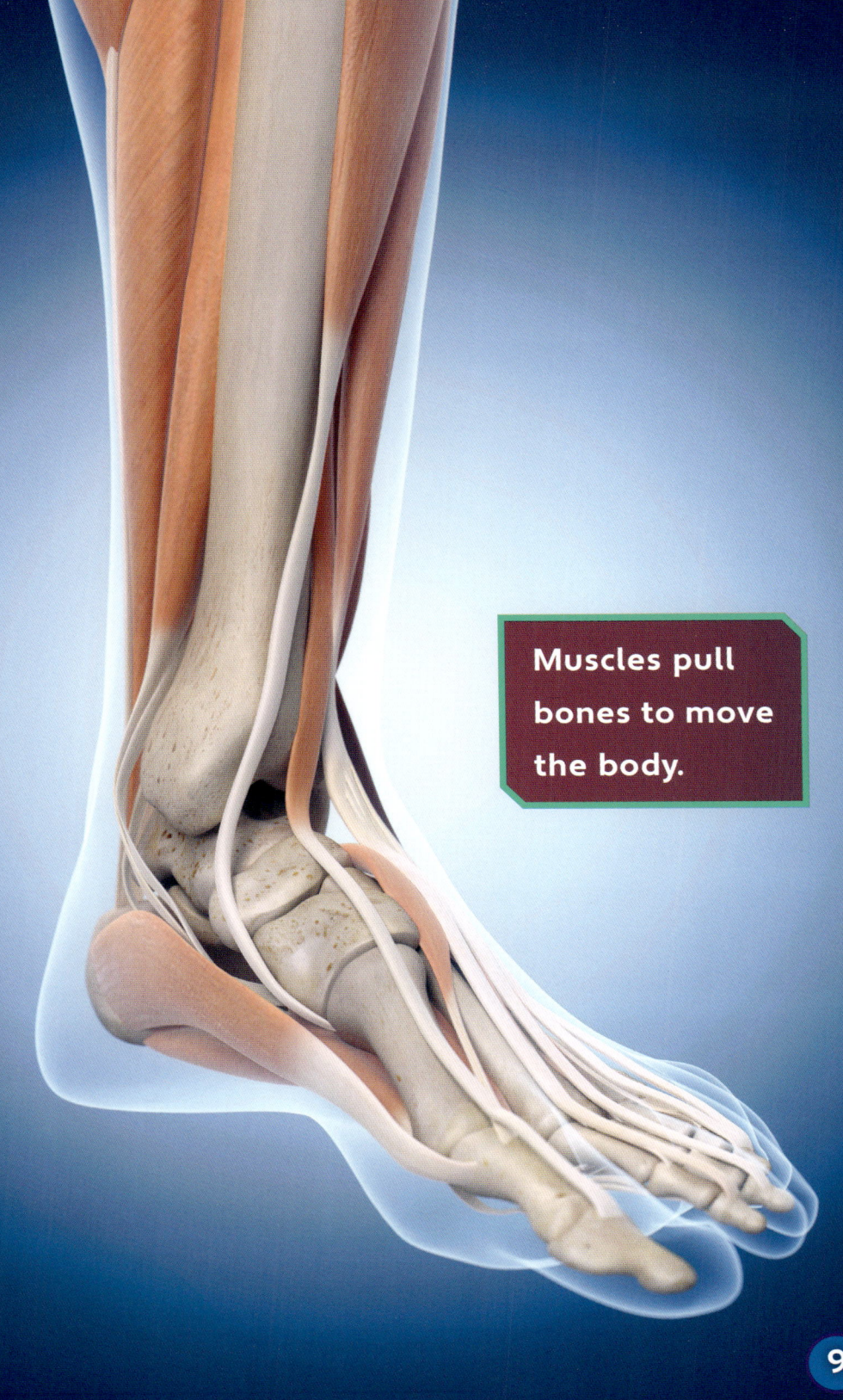

Muscles pull bones to move the body.

Strength includes both power and **endurance** (en-DUR-uhnss). Power is the most a body can push or lift for a short time. Endurance is how long the body can do something. Doing an activity for a longer period builds endurance.

Exercises that build power include push-ups and sit-ups. Running and swimming increase endurance. Some exercises can build both power and endurance.

We Heart Exercise

The second part of fitness involves heart and lung health. It is called **cardiovascular** fitness, or cardio. **Aerobic** (air-OH-bik) exercise helps with this. This exercise makes the heart beat faster. It can make a person breathe faster, too. This gets more oxygen to the lungs. Over time, aerobic exercise makes the heart and lungs stronger.

The word aerobic means with air. There are also **anaerobic** (an-er-ROH-bik) exercises. These are activities that do not need extra oxygen.

13

Exercise can have low, medium, and high levels of **intensity**. A higher intensity makes a person breathe harder and their heart beat faster. More oxygen goes into the body. Mixing levels keeps the body healthy and working well.

The same activity can often be done at different levels of intensity. Walking can be low or medium intensity.

Bend, Stretch, and Twist

The third part of fitness is flexibility (flek-suh-BIL-uh-tee). This includes bending and **stretching** muscles and **joints**. Stretching gets muscles ready for exercise. After exercise, it helps muscles recover. Yoga, dancing, and martial arts are good for flexibility.

Stretching increases a person's range of motion. This is how far the body can move in any direction. Having a high range of motion leads to fewer injuries.

A Brain Boost

Exercise does much more than just make the body healthy. It also helps the brain work better. As people exercise, their brains make **endorphins** (en-DOR-finz). These chemicals cause a person to feel good. Exercise also helps people sleep and learn better.

Doctors suggest young people should move their bodies for at least one hour every day. Most of this movement should be medium to high intensity.

Energy from exercise helps us pay attention in school.

19

Making Fitness Fit

Many people do more than one kind of fitness activity. This makes exercise more exciting. It helps them stay healthy in a fun way.

What might this look like? One day may focus on lifting weights to build strength. Another could involve running or biking for cardio health.

Most exercises can be **adapted** for different bodies. Sometimes, people need special equipment. This can help everyone get the same exercise benefits.

Doing exercises alone can get boring. Organized sports are fun to do with family or friends. Tennis, basketball, or skating are just a few choices. When a person is having fun, they are more likely to exercise.

Everyone's body and brain are different. It's important for each person to find exercises that feel good for them.

Take Care

Everyone needs exercise to stay healthy. But it's also possible to overdo it. Too much exercise can overwork the body. This may lead to injuries. Working too hard can also make people sick. Sometimes, the body needs a break.

Rest is very important for physical fitness. It lets the body recover from exercise or stress. Rest brings energy to the muscles and brain, too.

Being physically fit is important. Stay healthy by exercising every day. Do activities to make your muscles, heart, and lungs stronger. Be sure to move in different ways to stay flexible, too.

You only get one body. It's your job to take care of it.

Feeling anxious or scared about exercise may be a sign of needing help. Talk to a doctor, school nurse, or psychologist if you have these feelings.

How Exercise Helps the Body

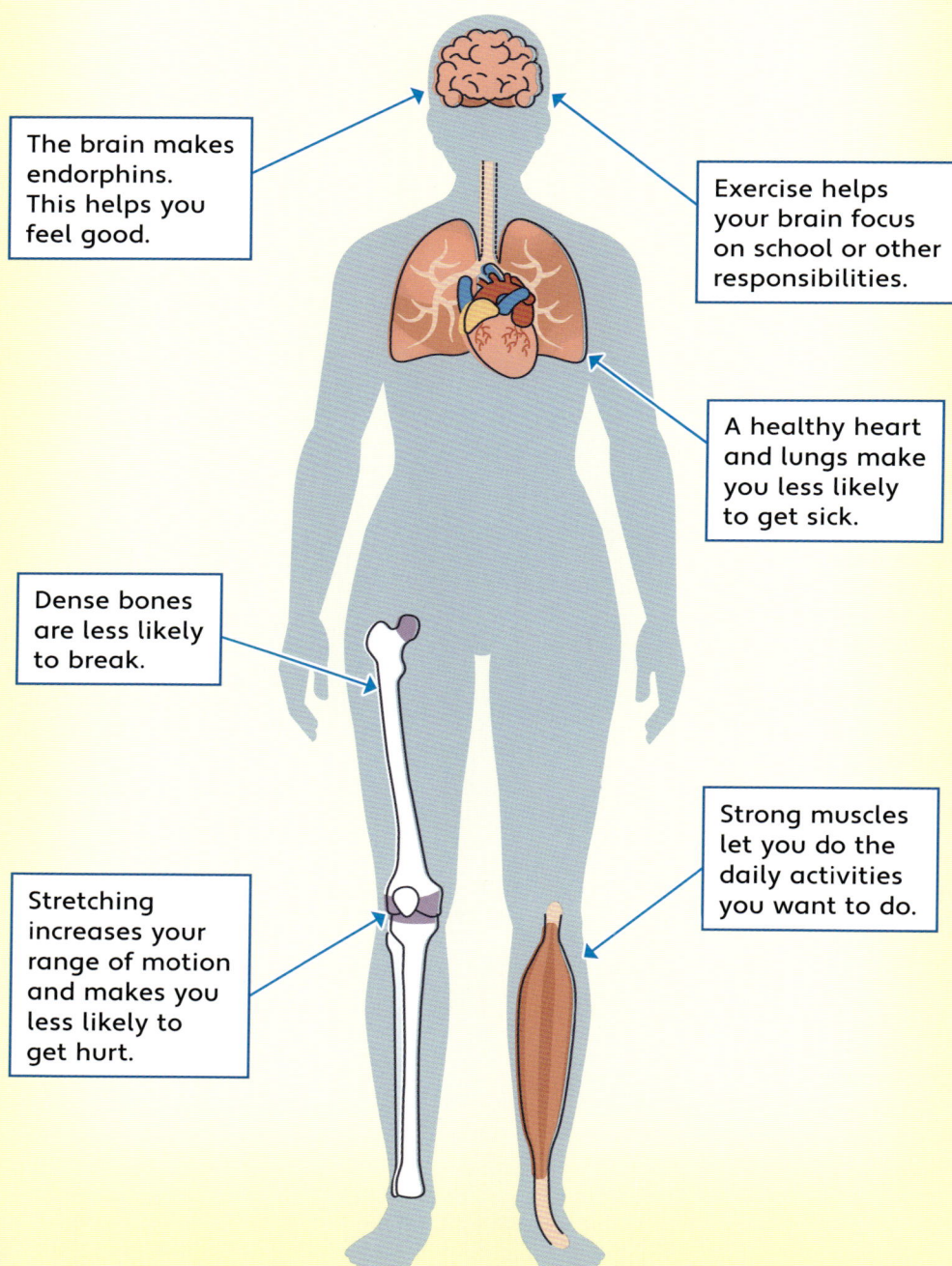

The brain makes endorphins. This helps you feel good.

Exercise helps your brain focus on school or other responsibilities.

A healthy heart and lungs make you less likely to get sick.

Dense bones are less likely to break.

Stretching increases your range of motion and makes you less likely to get hurt.

Strong muscles let you do the daily activities you want to do.

SilverTips for SUCCESS

★ SilverTips for REVIEW

Review what you've learned. Use the text to help you.

Define key terms

cardiovascular fitness   intensity
exercise   strength
flexibility

Check for understanding

What are the three parts of physical fitness?

Name the two measures of strength. Explain how they help the body.

In what ways does exercise help the brain?

Think deeper

How does physical fitness fit into your daily life? In what ways might you improve your physical fitness?

★ SilverTips on TEST-TAKING

- **Make a study plan.** Ask your teacher what the test is going to cover. Then, set aside time to study a little bit every day.

- **Read all the questions carefully.** Be sure you know what is being asked.

- **Skip any questions** you don't know how to answer right away. Mark them and come back later if you have time.

Glossary

adapted changed in order to fit the specific needs of an individual

aerobic with oxygen

anaerobic without oxygen

cardiovascular having to do with the heart and lungs

denser being thicker or more compact

endorphins brain chemicals that make people feel good

endurance the ability to do something for a long time

intensity how strong or powerful something is

joints places in the body where two bones connect

stress emotional or mental pressure

stretching exercising in a way that gently pulls muscles longer

Read More

Phillips-Bartlett, Rebecca. *Healthy Exercise (Live Well!).* Minneapolis: Bearport Publishing Company, 2024.

Snow, Peggy. *Active and Fit (Healthy and Happy).* Mankato, MN: Black Rabbit Books, 2025.

Wicks, Joe. *Fitter, Healthier, Happier! Your Guide to a Healthy Body and Mind.* New York: HarperCollins Publishers, 2024.

Learn More Online

1. Go to **FactSurfer.com** or scan the QR code below.

2. Enter "**Physical Fitness**" into the search box.

3. Click on the cover of this book to see a list of websites.

Index

About the Author

Ashley Kuehl is an editor and writer specializing in nonfiction for young people. She lives in Minneapolis, MN.